Enterprise, Inc.

Enterprise, Inc.

poems

Charles Sweetman

Dream Horse Press
California

Portions of FASB Concepts Statement No. 2, *Qualitative
Characteristics of Accounting Information*, copyright by the Financial
Accounting Standards Board, 401 Merritt 7, PO Box 5116, Norwalk,
CT 06856-5116. Reproduced with permission.

Library of Congress Cataloging-in-Publication Data:

Sweetman, Charles
        Enterprise, Inc.
                p.   cm

                ISBN 978-0-9821155-1-0
                1. Poetry

10 9 8 7 6 5 4 3 2 1

First Edition

Cover: "Damariscotta Dream" by Lynda Lehmann,
        http://www.lyndalehmann.com/

Acknowledgments

Thanks to the editors of the publications where these poems appeared in slightly different forms and titles.

GSU Review: "Recipe for Disaster"
Gingko Tree Review: "The Life and Times of Jay Brewer, Performance Consultant"
River Styx: "The Illusionist"

Thanks to C. J. Sage, for selecting the following poems as winners of the 2007 Dream Horse Chapbook Prize:

> "Something Big"
> "Jake"
> "Tipsy Garden Gnomes"
> "A Question of Principles"
> "Gig 'Em Ags"
> "Gold Rush"
> "Ollie Ollie Outs In Free!"
> "Second Act: A New Leaf"
> "The Future: A History"
> "To Staff"
> "Shiners"
> "Invasion of the Topless Dancers"
> "Portrait of Jim Gerwitz as an Early Retiree"
> "The UnAmerican Dream of Paul Martinez"
> "Departmental"
> "Renee Departs"

I am indebted in a real and immediate way to Lisa Ampleman, Matt Fluharty, Jeff Hamilton, Lisa Pepper, Terry Quinn, Shane Seely, Jason Sommer, and Corinne Taff who have read and made better so many of these poems. I would also like to thank Marshall Klimasewiski, David Lawton, Carl Phillips, Noel Sloboda, and Jonathan Bolton for invaluable help with, and interest in, my writing. I am grateful to J.P. Dancing Bear for seeing the potential of this book at an early stage and for putting his name and press behind it. And finally, I thank my family for unfailing support, especially Beth and Claire whose good humor and good sense make our home a great place to write as well as a place to leave writing alone.

Contents

for Pat Sweetman

I.

Information about a particular enterprise gains greatly in usefulness if it can be compared with similar information about other enterprises and with similar information about the same enterprise for some other period or some other point in time.

—"Comparability and Consistency"
  Statement of Financial Accounting Concepts No. 2 (FASB)

Something Big

Half of us in Internal Audit at Enterprise
were working on something big. Accounting
just paid the bills, you understand.
Jones studied astrology with Madam Katrina.
Leilany tangoed. I'd have my novel someday,
an audit of the American Dream, and I wrote
my observations and conversations in a ledger
at my desk. Dorma's passion was greeting cards,
drawn and rhymed under her pseudonym *Dear Heart*.
One night, in the middle of Graphic Art 205,
Dorma was discovered by a boutique owner.
We began waiting for the day she would strike out
on her own. And waiting. Supporting her
as best we could, but talking among ourselves
about the downturn in public sentimentality,
the trouble it spelled for the greeting card industry.
Then, Karmody, the marathoner, got news
the deal with the boutique was off. We jumped
into action, baking casseroles and pies. Gracie made
Dorma a Mardi Gras King cake from her new line
of desserts. That was how sorry we were.

Jake

"Everything's Jake," Gerwitz used to call out
over the cubicle tops on quiet afternoons
when deadlines oppressed and rush hour eluded.
He stole the line, he told me, from an old gangster
flick when a racketeer shrugs off a close-call
that would have blown the gang's cover.
But let's face it, Witz in his polyester
slacks and clip-on tie could never pull off
two-tone-shoe cool, let alone wear a straw
porkpie at a rakish angle. They finally caught up
to him during the Early-Retirement phase
of the new Redesign. After he'd gone,
when afternoons grew eerily quiet, one of us
would be moved to say, "Everything's Jake."
And someone would reply, "Sure Thing," or,
"You Bet." Oh it was still on, all right. Still on.

Second Act: A New Leaf

(Take One)

From her calls for action and vows to cut
her losses, I gathered Renee was directing
her next move, casting me, her unofficial
biographer, as the test audience for a plot twist
that would resolve her contradictions
and focus futuristic projections
—zooming past what hadn't panned out
until her dialogue took on its signature
surrealism. "To be quite honest,"
she would begin, and go on to lie fantastically
about the discipline she had recovered,
the riveting purpose with which she was
rededicating her career, now that she no longer
kept a ledger of mistakes, only outtakes.

(Take Two)

"That's the last time I drink upside-down
margaritas in a dental chair," Renee said,
proclaiming Saturday part of a bygone era
of command performances and desk-top
romances that had flourished during her reign
as Fabulous Party Girl at Enterprise.
But the idealism of a Caesar
salad at her desk with unsweetened
tea and the latest quarterlies struck me
as the ceremonial gesture of a Romantic
Age already in its twilight. In the crunch
of Romaine leaves you could hear
the Neo-Booze period marching toward
Wednesday's happy hour at Waves.

The Big Dogs of Dressel & Fitzweiller

In January, the external auditors from D&F
returned and resumed their place
in the north-west executive suite. Kotch, Taft,
Deford and a new guy, Hooper. I waved.
And as they sauntered over I dropped
to the carpet and rolled on my back,
knees bent, arms held close to my chest.
I kept still while they nosed around,
sniffing my wallet for new money,
my tie for the old confidence. Not that
they had anything to prove. They weren't
the one who'd left prestigious D&F
to work at one of the clients.
But these reunions had a form.
This was how it was done. Satisfied,
Kotch helped me up. Deford patted
my back. Taft even sparred a little.
I didn't have to say, "glad *I'm* not facing
another long busy season." They
didn't go on about the fast track. They
were good guys. It was good to see them.

The Illusionist

Facing another year of number-crunching
servitude under the credit-snatching
E. Forest Greg, Rita called a headhunter.
Rich Ringle had just the opportunity for her:
a fast-growing *Fortune* 500 with great fringes,
competitive salary, and innovative people.
She agreed to lunch, but warned she wouldn't
become another Gretchen Schmidt, pigeonholed
at thirty. "Trust me," he said. "You want to hear this."

After Greek salad and jasmine tea, Ringle
ordered their table bussed and put on
white, sequined gloves. He set a black top hat
on the ivory tablecloth and began placing
things in the hat, like a number-two ranking
in Who's Who of Financial Services, skyrocketing
earnings, holistic mentoring by one of three
Personal Performance Consultants (PPCs).
An industry-leading stock purchase plan
and an 18 floor miniature golf course
were other facets of this work-hard, play-hard
culture with branches in Brussels and London.

Next, with a sparkling smile, Ringle drew
feathers from Rita's cap, presenting each
in its best light before placing it in the hat.
There were her immaculate transcripts,
a semester in Florence, three volleyball
state championships, two early promotions,
and four blue ribbon citations as a volunteer
for the Special Olympics. Ringle added
a letter of recommendation from Rita's
first manager, Oak Hall, who called her
the pearl from a grain of sand.

Finally—nothing up this sleeve or that—Ringle

reached into the hat and drew forth a mother-
of-pearl career with immaculate feathers
and blinking blue eyes. He let it flutter-balance
on his finger while Rita caught her breath, then
extended his hand to her. For a moment,
Rita wondered about busy season overtime.
But she held her tongue. Any doubt, she knew,
and it might all vanish as if it had never been.

Tipsy Garden Gnomes

Lonny's oldest boy broke his neck boating
Friday night and was still in intensive care
Monday. Gracie, Lonny's neighbor, told us
about the kid's less-than-sober high school
career, how Saturday mornings she'd find
her garden gnomes hugging beer cans,
her plastic pink flamingoes roosting
in her tall oak trees. ("God knows how
those boys climbed in that condition.")
"Oh, it sounds harmless," said Karmody,
chuckling—"A young man needs an outlet
for all that energy." But Gracie shouted,
"The corporate ladder isn't made of aluminum
beer cans, Charles Karmody!" What looked
like another scathing comment rising inside
her became a sob, and she turned away.
After she had passed the filing cabinets,
Karmody told me that Gracie taught the kid
piano until junior year when he dropped
lessons for football, a decision Lonny supported.
"She was a good influence on the boy,"
Karmody said, wiping his eye with a knuckle—
"On us all really. And it's true what she says
about the ladder. Don't I know it . . . but
it isn't climbed by garden gnomes. Someone
should tell Gracie—garden gnomes don't climb."

A Question of Principles

"What would you rather be," Albert asked
at lunch after the tough, but constructive,
performance evaluation I'd given him—
"best player on a losing team or second-
stringer on the state champions?" I'd only
ever played tennis in high school, fifth seed
on a so-so squad, and a big challenge
match still played over and over in my memory.
"Best player," I said. He smiled that smug
grin of his—"Exactly why you'll always be
second string." I was impressed by that—
just the kind of clear, concise, completely
insulting retort that made you aware
of his talent for individuality, the discipline
behind his obscure championship run.

Portrait of Hooper as a Drama Minor
Pulling an All-nighter for the Finance Exam

Return on Investment (ROI) tests management's efficiency.
Capital is a scarce resource and must be used efficiently.
Observe the relationship of short-term assets to liabilities
with a test known as the **current ratio**. Currently, Hooper
is said to be inefficient when he plays Biff Loman
in the University's production *Death of a Salesman*.

Tangible assets have physical substance, e.g. diamonds.
Intangible assets lack physical substance and are hard
to value because **evidence** of their existence is elusive.
"What happened to the old confidence?" Happy asks Biff
in the school's dramatic production *Death of a Salesman*.

Because they hinge on estimates of future operating results,
capital budgeting decisions are complicated.
"Why am I trying to become what I don't want to be?"
Biff asks himself. "The doors of your life are wide open!"
say campus recruiters who invest in seniors with high
grade points, otherwise known as **earnings potential**.

Happy is confused but **hard-skinned**, refusing to admit
he is lost. Biff shouts, "Pop, I'm nothing! **Nothing**, Pop,"
sinking Willy's dreams for his success. However regrettable,
a **write-off** can enable change, and so a **cost** that has been
irrevocably incurred is called **sunk** because it is **irrelevant**

to **future** decisions, however **disappointing to Pop**.
More relevant are **Opportunity Costs**: the benefits
forgone when choosing one **course of action** over another.
These costs tend to be **subjective**, for example,
the **happiness Biff** foregoes when unable to **say who he is**.
Opportunity costs **are not recorded** in the accounting records.

Gold Rush

During happy hour, Duke kept asking us how
much we were paid and how we were ever
going to amass enough for early retirement.
Beer and our evasions only made him more
insistent. To change the subject, Renee asked if
anybody'd seen a good movie lately. Duke had.
One about the California Gold Rush. He bored
us with a story of greed and suspicion until
Renee exposed his plot as a thinly-veiled allegory
of our department—each of us staking claim
to a nugget of talent and mining it for all it
was worth. Duke, she said, was the honest
but naïve prospector whose plot gets jumped.
She herself was the storekeeper making a mint
off the miners; Aldy was the alcoholic preacher;
Marcie, the Chinese laborer. For a moment
I feared being type-cast as the sheriff in the pocket
of the rich banker, so I was pleased when Renee
put me down as the prostitute with a heart of gold.

Guest Speaker Rip Calhoun and the Servants of the Soul

"Back in my own salad days I kept an eye out
for a mentor. One day, Vivian Mulcahy took me
aside and said when the time came, I should insist
on a corner office, *even if* I had to take a pay-cut
to get it. She was then the newly installed head
of Advertising, and this was exactly what
I'd been waiting for: the 'big advice' moment—
The streets are like tea leaves, she said,
rolling her chair to look down at the wide avenues
below. *They tell the perceptive reader what's next.*
Today, I see fraud. Little ants scurrying to the next lie.
It may be the preposterous embezzlement
they've contemplated for months, or just the claim
they want a Ribsy's garden salad and not the world
famous Dill Cheddar Burger. Back at their desks,
they won't understand their growing dissatisfaction.
And when they feel the urge to pretend
they're someone else, we'll be there with an identity
and an invoice. . . . While she said this,
I'd been watching her right hand. It never stopped
smoothing her skirt, twirling her pen, poking
the ice in her glass. *Hands are the servants of the soul,*
my father used to say. Well, and you can quote me
on this, I knew right then, you've got to keep
your eye on the ball, even as you look inside
yourself for the courage to swing."

Broadway Seifert

At times like this—the heady talk of historic
football teams wafting over the beige partitions,
mixing with the sound of telephones and ten-key
tape—Seifert felt the cubicles kept him honest
in two ways. First—in rolling up his sleeves
and going toe to toe with Karmody, a hard-nosed
and well-spoken but naïve guy from the Bronx
who couldn't brag about his beloved Jets this year
but nevertheless maintained a store-house
of East-Coast-centric set pieces, like the one proclaiming
Broadway Joe Namath the Godfather of the modern-
day quarterback (a semi-outrageous, though not
unfounded and certainly colorful, assertion)
—first, Seifert had to admit he enjoyed himself immensely,
like a kid almost, crafting confident claims
in the privacy of his cube and then sending
them along with compelling support over the walls
to make their way in the democratic space above.

But second, second he had to acknowledge
that to outsiders like Duke, two cubes over
—who didn't know a cut-back from a crack-block,
but knew crack-pot when he heard it (and in this way
resembled a young Seifert himself)—it was all
ridiculous hooha. "Tell me you didn't really just say
you were deducting *points* from Fran Tarkington
because he threw *wobbly* sprials," was all Duke
had to say for Seifert to see himself from Duke's eyes
—a blue blazer and gray slacked, forty-two year old
CPA, formerly of Rice & Feller where,
for godsakes, he'd be partner by now if he'd had
the guts to stake his claim, or at least manager
of this internal audit department if he hadn't dropped
out of the race, escaping into bowl games and box scores—
and for Seifert to admit the pertinence of the point

(if not excuse the impertinence of the speaker)
and to blush behind his beige partition,
like that time he made out with the fat girl
on the couch in the middle of the frat house.

A Wildcatter for Our Time

We were eating the free oysters at Crumley's
when in walks a guy with an Armani suit,
cowboy boots, shades, and gray hair down
to his collar in the back. Renee thought he was
the lead singer from that old band *The Caustics*,
but the bartender said, no, he was Klip Schoendist,
senior partner at Rice & Feller. The CPA who
almost single-handedly wrote the FASB
on accounting for natural gas reserves. The guy
who started Old Wellington when Bellerive kicked
him out for doing donuts on the putting green.
The Splendid Klipper. As he walked past,
we all raised our cosmopolitans and poured
them in the pretzel dishes, humming "Born to Be
Wild." It was the closest any of us had been
to a real accounting rebel.

The Second and Final Meeting of the Self-Improvement Book Club

"If you're the CFO of a sinking ship,
which would you rather your CEO had:
golden handcuffs or a golden parachute?"
was Ray's question, and it divided us according
to where we sided with our first two books,
Managerial Moxie in Sun Tzu's Art of War
or *Darwin, Alive and Well on Wall Street.*
The Sun Tzus were first to organize, insisting
that the illusion of commitment would prompt
a bail-out strategy. But the Darwinians adapted
quickly: "Who'd want a CEO who wasn't fit
to survive?" Duke, as usual, tried to move us
onto MBA turf, saying the question was another
version of *who would win in a fight: organization
man or reorganization man*? Marcie said it wasn't
any such version. Renee, who was not a fan
of either book and a pacifist, said there were too
many variables to decide—which was how
books like these co-existed atop the bestseller list
in the first place. "Then what was the bottom line?"
we said—"How were you supposed to create
a leadership plan from that?" Discussion
stalled until Renee motioned we adjourn for beers
at Ale House, where it was felt we should
discuss only real-world scenarios.

God-Forsaken Desert of Zoysia

"Up with Zoysia, down with Fescue!"
Kyle called across the noisy patio
at his college graduation party. I'd recently
bought the house next door, and we'd skewer
suburban life over his dad's picket fence.
Lawn care was his favorite target. Praising
the rapid-spreading, weed-choking but early-
browning Zoysia over the shade-tolerant
Tall Fescue, he meant *we're the only ones,*
you and I, in this god-forsaken desert of lush
grasses and blue swimming pools, who feel
the needs of the soul. Kyle's young and a bit
sentimental. I held up my plastic cocktail
cup in a toast. But I was put off later when,
in what can only be described as a protest
against his fast-narrowing middle-class future,
Kyle scraped a key across the fender of every
car in his father's driveway. I happened to know
Mrs. Johanson could ill afford the deductible
on her Bonneville. I advised her to report it
as a collision, and I stuck a note on my fridge:
"Speak to Kyle about the feelings of serenity
promoted by grass with its yearly cycle,
sign of our countryside heritage."

Ollie Ollie Outs in Free!

Sundays, the Midwesterners in the Houston
office drove to my ranch house out
in Sugarland to barbeque and play games
on my wide lawn. Once, during Kick the Can,
Albert leapt the picket fence and kept running.
He didn't come back—even when we called
Ollie Ollie Outs in Free. It started getting dark
and hard to see. Albert was sulking somewhere.
There were no fireflies or cicadas. Tamara finished
washing the ice cream bowls and from the window
over the sink called our names into the humid
night. We came in, put on our pajamas,
and brushed our teeth before Aldy said
it was time to drive back to the condos.
Monday, Albert's manager called asking
his whereabouts. I suggested she look behind
the Chevron Tower but keep a sharp eye
on the freeways, especially I-45 North.

Double Wing Right 28 Power Sweep—Fake

"In one of my daydreams," I told Brewer,
the corporation's ace performance consultant,
"I'm a fullback for the Dallas Cowboys,
shoulder-pads stacked high, hands on my knees.
At the snap, I break right, catch the lateral high,
and slide in behind my guards, as they pull out."
I tucked a binder in the crook of my arm.
"There's this zone I'm in . . . this zone where—"
"Good!" said Brewer sitting atop his mahogany
desk—"Touchdown! See. You're finally getting it!"
 "No," I said—"No. I never actually cut
up-field. In the dream, I keep running sideways
behind my guards, and the sideline recedes."

Brewer frowned. Then he nodded—"Of course!"
and popped off his desk—"What we have here
is a classic case of *achievement fear*. And, you,
my friend, are a staller, happy to live in that bubble
of pure intention just before the fracas at the line
of scrimmage." He snapped his fingers—
"Let's try some visualization—a *projection scenario*.
Close your eyes. Imagine the same game,
same play. I'll be QB this time. This time I *fake*
the lateral. You tuck to decoy and then snake
your way into the endzone for a pass. Okay, on three.
On three, tell me exactly what you see——hut hut *hut!*"

"They're big," I said, eyes closed, shoulder-faking
left—"One guy bumps me, sniffing for
the ball . . . lets me go. The safety sees me—but
. . . he's letting me go, too! I'm wide open! Here
in the corner! Throw it! Throw it. . . . I'm. . . .
What're you waiting for?" I opened my eyes.
Brewer was jogging in place. His face

was flushed and his breath came heavily.
 "Sorry," he said, wiping his brow—"The rush
was too strong. Had to keep it myself. Faked that big
bastard right out of his jockstrap on my way in!"
Brewer spiked an imaginary ball—"Boom."
Then he took his seat and said calmly, "We scored,
you understand. It's a team win. Teamwork.
No way I get in without your decoy."

The Winners of This World

Della's center admin. cubicle was perfect
for eavesdropping on the loose-lipped
conversations about the lottery. Co-workers
would practically broadcast their combos—
anniversary of a dog's death, birthdays
doubled backwards. When she heard
a good strategy, she'd file it in her desk.
Sometimes she hedged, ticketing their
numbers as well as her own. She felt
a rhythm, a pattern, possibly even a logic
to providence, and she was closing in
on what it was and how it worked.

She'd learned to resist the high priced
coffee at the Stop-N-Go, however
convenient. Did without her cigarillos
when the budget demanded. That was what you
had to understand about Della Millhouse.
She wasn't afraid to put in her dues.
—Abe Lincoln lost something like fifty
elections. Edison's bulbs blew thousands
of times. How many strikeouts did Aaron
endure on his way to 755? —Go right ahead
and tell her the odds were against her, that
she was more likely to get struck by lightning
and run over on the same day. That only
made her work twice as hard. "The winners
of this world," read the bumper sticker
tacked to her cube, "make their own luck."

The Parable of the Talentless

The night he was passed over for senior,
Albert held forth at the Ale House
and spoke thus: "The president of an oil
drilling firm was going on a long junket.
He awarded his three vice presidents a bonus
to invest in their departments as each saw fit.
When the president returned to settled accounts,
the first said, *Sir, I know you're a man who plays*
favorites. I therefore gave the money to your
nephew with the hope you will both like me.
Here is a picture of us at dinner. —Well done!
said the President. *Keep it up and you'll be*
like family to me. Likewise, the second
approached and said, *Sir, you've proven it's*
not what you know but who you know.
I therefore spent the money wooing lobbyists
in Washington. Here are the bar tabs,
ball game receipts, and a list of gifts.
—Well done! said the president. *Maybe we'll*
get help in our waste-dumping trial.
The third approached. *Sir, not everyone*
can be as lucky as you, who reaps huge
personal reward from the work of others.
So I devised an incentive plan to recognize
our most innovative workers. —You crafty
and wicked VP, said the president. *You could*
have at least let Me unveil it with customary
pomp and circumstance. To the other VPs he said,
Show this man the door, and let him gnash his teeth.
Split his department and run it as you see fit.
—Amen I say to you," concluded Albert,
"The first shall be last, the last first."

Quick Studies

1. The Cowboy

After just a little practice on the impressionable
Midwesterners, Aldy developed a personality
indistinguishable from the Klipper prototype:
the tall, nonchalant, womanizer cowboy, bemused
by the big city but comfortable in its fast lanes,
living on the edge of his credit card. For a twist
he added a big, blue boat of a Cadillac. Floating
down Westheimer Friday night, young set
of the office in tow, he was the grand marshal
of his own gaudy parade.

2. The Shark

The best of the poker set, Karmen claimed
she had a counting system for black jack
and another for Texas hold'em. She was going
to take it to Vegas and live out in the neon
desert with her rescue-dog, One-eyed-Jack.
And damn if she didn't do it! Within the year
she sent pictures of her ranch house with a view
of the mountains and the glittery Vegas skyline.
The casino that hired her as assistant controller
paid for the move, the downstroke on her new
home, everything. We'd had our pockets picked
again. Vintage Shark, even sharper out West.

3. Lily Carmichael, Slalomist Extraordinaire

"They say you're not corner office material

until you've skied the Alps with Grant Thurston.
This could be a power play by Thurston's cronies
(who're losing their control of the promotions
committee), or it could be a misdirection ploy
by Serena Jackson and her up-and-comers
(who like nothing better than to bust Thurston's
prodigies on frivolous junkets). So I ask you:
with the glass ceiling looming just above her head,
can a girl afford not to practice her slalom?"

Cafeteria Big Time

Big Jeminez, the flap-jack king, called in sick
for a week, and management brought in
four cooks in short order, each more famous
than the last, starting with Keith Caruthers, aka
The Dolphin. After him came the Gizzard
brothers, who slung egg wash as liberally
as I'd ever seen it done, and, out of retirement,
Mave "The Rave" Johansen, famous for
"The Shift"—her 48 consecutive hours that kept
the place stable during the layoff scare
from Black Tuesday to Cinco de Mayo. With that
kind of talent in the wings, I wondered where
Jeminez ever got the balls to try out down there,
back when he was just the flap-jack wizard
and didn't have his red spatula.

Hardball

"DROP IT!" shouted a Legion of Doom mother,
whose ten-year old had popped up to Dorma's Pirate
son behind first. The fly, a real can of corn,
hung up for Johnny, but he flinched, dropped it,
and allowed the go-ahead run—who hadn't bothered
tagging up—to score. Dorma's throat clenched,
but she soothed: "It's okay, Johnny! You'll get it
next time." Then she called out, "Hey, Ump,
how about sportsmanship!" The umpire lifted his mask
and scolded the Legion, but while he whisked the plate,
the Legion huddled and smirked, scorning
Dorma's squeamishness as so much non-binding
arbitration called for by an investigative
committee without any real, hard evidence.
And everyone knew it.

Lonny Harper and the Authority of Success

"His mother tells me I shouldn't ride the kid
so hard. I'm the ogre because he sulks
and slams the door after so-called polishing
the car. It looks clean to me, she says.
She's thinking road grime. I'm talking character.
By the time I was sixteen, I drove a combine!
Mucked pigsties. *And look*, she says, *you've made it
possible for him not to slave all summer.*
Be thankful you've created a better life, she says.
She's looking from the kitchen. I'm looking
into the future. How's Marty going to learn
the value of hard work if he leaves dried wax
in every crevice? If a job's worth doing,
it's worth doing right. I mean, am I right
or am I right? Dream all you want about self-esteem.
Character is doing what you don't want to do.
The difference between success and failure is
the difference between a toothbrush and a chamois."

High Noon

"Can I start you with something to drink,
gentlemen?" said their waiter on the patio
of Carmen's, high noon. Robert deferred
to Harold, the regional manager who'd flown
him to Houston for an interview. Harold ordered
a gin gimlet and glanced at Robert as if to say,
"How do you like them apples?" Luckily,
Robert had read *The Intrepid Interview*,
which sensibly advised that while most
interview luncheons are drier than a Baptist
revival in the desert, they can be as dry
as a three-olive martini if you notice certain
verbal and/or non-verbal cues. Robert guessed
that Harold's gimlet was not *The False Foot
Forward* gambit but, rather, *The Stand-Up Guy*
routine. He countered with an Oldfashioned.
Harold nodded approvingly at his menu.

Munching bread between answers, Robert
half-expected a *Yes-Man Change-Up*,
a question so irrational as to constitute a trap
for the overly compliant. Instead, Harold went
for a cross between a *Guard-Downer* and a
Green-Lighter, offering the wine list to Robert.
Robert chose a Sauvignon Blanc to go with their
salmon Caesar, and Harold smiled openly
and ordered another round—to which Robert raised
his Oldfashioned with a nod and killed it.
Robert himself suggested the carafe of port
to go with bread pudding, though he only sipped.
And it was Rob who supported Harry across
the parking lot while Harry sang "Fly me
to the Moon." In the driver's seat, Rob hoped
he'd sign a contract this time tomorrow.
But he remained sensibly aware that he'd overdone
it and might draw instead the dreaded *Ink Blotto*.

The Jumping Marlins of the Caribbean

If you were going to the Grand Canyon,
Seifert had already camped at the bottom
and packed out on a mule. Think you had
put in some overtime lately—you should
have been in Seifert's department during
the "Easter Parade," as he called it,
when they worked seven straight Sundays
and practically all got walking pneumonia.
When Duke finally got his new truck, Seifert
bought the same exact model a week later,
slightly used so he didn't blow twenty percent
just driving it off the lot. "That guy would tell
Gandhi how to pray," Duke complained.
"He's a topper, all right," said Jones—
"You can't beat him."

But Duke was nothing if not a competitor.
Not long after the truck incident, Seifert
came over for lunch, and Duke announced
he was going deep sea fishing in Key West.
It was probably a bluff, and Seifert rose
to the bait. "Sun-Coast Expeditions, right?"
"Hold it, Mister," said Duke, "we know
darn well you've never been to the Keys."
"Who said I had?" said Seifert—"Buddy
of mine went. Worst time of his life. Rotten
equipment, choppy water, terrible guide. Marlins
been fished out down there for a decade.
You hook more than a piece of seaweed,
it's just sheer dumb luck." Duke stood there
open-mouthed while Seifert took a great bite
out of his burrito. Jones just clucked—"Bad
money after good. Bad money after good."

The Millionaire Next Door

Martinez was rich. Something about a real
estate deal in Austin, and it drove people
crazy. He'd pull up at 7:55 in his green
Chevy, and someone would say "If I had
his money, you wouldn't see my sorry ass
in here at eight . . . or nine, or ten." Mondays
were worst. "Every day," went Duke's gripe—
"he eats hard-boiled eggs, chips, and a pear.
No broiled chicken. No brownie. No iced tea."
Duke belonged to the live-for-the-moment
camp who felt you had to eat more ice cream
and walk barefoot to be happy. Others felt
you could never be too rich and believed living
in Florida was the way to get more from life.
Once, Gracie said, "there are lots of Martinezes
walking around in sensible shoes with fat
bank accounts and cheap suits who've never
even been to Florida." It was too much for Jones.
"What're they waiting for?" he exploded—
"The Dow Jones to get down there first?
What's the point of having it all if you're
just like everyone else?" Gracie just smiled.
"That's it right there," she said—"You can't
fathom the rich. A strange and glamorous race."

II.

Information can make a difference to decisions by improving decision makers' capacities to predict or by confirming or correcting their earlier expectations. Usually, information does both at once, because knowledge about the outcomes of actions already taken will generally improve decision makers' abilities to predict the results of similar future actions. Without a knowledge of the past, the basis for prediction will usually be lacking. Without an interest in the future, knowledge of the past is sterile.

—"Feedback Value and Predictive Value as Components of Relevance"
Statement of Financial Accounting Concepts No. 2 (FASB)

The Future: A History
as told by Renee Turner

The Future of Enterprise, declared CEO
Troller in his first Annual Report, was its people.
Later, during The Hard Reality, it turned
out that some people were not the future—
in fact jeopardized it—leading to layoffs
so large they were called Downsizing. Loyalty
became a thing of the past, replaced by portable
benefits, which were light enough to carry
out the door if you weren't pulling your weight.
Night classes became the rage as workers
who hadn't kept up their computer skills
scrambled to get certificates on their résumés.
Human Resources rolled out policies like Flex-Time
and held 10K runs in the new gym. Manufacturing
said floating holidays would increase productivity
plus pay for themselves in foregone sick days.
Meanwhile, technology was making everyone
more efficient. And Efficiency was the Key.
But it wasn't everything, critics complained—
what about Quality?—hadn't The Hard Reality
been followed by The Commitment to Quality?
Quality was fine, said the new flock of MBAs,
so long as it accompanied Growth because
Joe Investor had to send his kid to college.
Analysts predicted that whatever black ink came
from sudden Growth, red was sure to follow.
Visionary Cliff Anderson was tapped to replace
Troller as CEO, and he said if The Sky was
to become The Limit again, Enterprise had to return
to Core Strengths. First and foremost of these
was its creative, talented people.

Gig 'Em Ags

I looked into the conference room to ask
Duke about a voucher sample. At first I didn't see
him. Only heard heavy breathing. Then I saw
the back of his red head bobbing up
and down behind the table. "Forty-seven, forty-
eight, forty-nine—" "What the hell, Duke?"
I said. He said it was tradition at A&M
for cadets to do push-ups after every Aggie
touchdown. It was something he did now when
he finished an audit segment under budget.
Maybe *that* was it, I thought. *Pride. Spirit.*
I hadn't gone to a big state school, just a liberal
arts college with a lousy basketball team. No
cheerleaders. All I had were my grandpa's Irish
jokes, a recipe for half-baked Alaska, "Mighty
Fortress" and a handful of other Protestant
fight songs. That same week, I glued root beer
candies to my calendar on the wall—a kind of
advent tree—opening one each day to count
down the audit. But what was the use?
Where was the pageantry?

Shiners

Albert had a cast of co-workers who'd become
super-villains in his personal office comic book.
He called them Shiners. Each possessed and abused
a special power. Normally mild-mannered Tad
Aldridge could stretch his personality two, even three
times life size, until he became Aldy, The Man,
and you either cozied up or were squeezed out.
Duke saw right through people but was blind
to his own naked ambitions. Tamara, the most beautiful
woman in the world, dated the biggest assholes
on the face of the planet and had no use for old
classmates who knew her when she was just Tammy
from Ohio and didn't have her vermillion cape.
Albert spent hours fathoming their weaknesses
and disputing their successes in a series of dark,
smoky capers at the Ale House, where he matched
wits with various Shiner defenders. One night,
Marcie said, "Why do you take it so personally?
They probably aren't thinking about you at all."
She was right, Albert thought. *He was invisible!*
From then on, around Shiners, Albert would float
quips under his breath, lob sarcastic rejoinders
from across the room. Each time from farther away,
practicing for the day he would vanish completely.

National Take-Your-Inner-Child-to-Work Day

The pieces on Renee's marble chessboard
were jumbled. "I knocked them over
carrying groceries," she said—"and I didn't
have the heart to set them up. Now they
just fraternize, make-out, loiter, reminisce.
That queen there with her head propped
on the stomach of the bishop has been
cantering horseback all day in the old forest.
Picking berries." Renee was fishing for keys
in that enormous purse of hers. I was thinking
this explained a lot—possibly she'd swished
through the office Monday in a plaid skirt
and saddle shoes, saying from now on
she was working like she did in school,
when she painted page after page with Fluorescent
highlighters and grades were just a game.
"Has the bishop said anything about
money?" I said, sympathetically, bitterly,
pretentiously—"how it changes things?"-
unwittingly throwing away what chance I had
to be her knight in shining armor.

Portrait of Jim Gerwitz as an Early Retiree

She was still there when he peeked
over the sports page—the plump
woman in blue running warm ups.
He got the feeling she was watching
as he left the kitchen table for coffee,
and he wanted more than ever to say,
"Get you a cup of java, Jonesy?" But Jones
was well out of earshot now. This strange
woman sat next to him on the way
to the hardware store, shadowed him
through Tools and Paint, followed him
all the way home before he gave her
the slip at the den. There, pretending
to paint the trim, he called headquarters:
"She's in there, Jones! I just know it,
waiting." "Don't panic," soothed
Jones—"Now, I want you to look out
the west corner window and tell me
what you see." Gerwitz peeked—"It's her!
There through the bay window! Making
sandwiches." "Then it's as I suspected.
You're going to have to go in there
and face her. Find out who she is."

The Burgundy Fez

Lily Charmichael was the first woman
ever to reach the Inner Sanctum
of the Minnehaha Civic Leadership Club.
Even the club's cynical organ of gossip,
The Vicious Circle, grease-skidded her
at two-to-one for the office of High
Fellowship. But after Lily hung fire
at the Mayor's re-election ball, all bets
were off. The whole club went Full Tilt.
While the High Fellows met to decide
her fate, The Vicious Circle convened
a special Fallout session. One suspects
they savored the delicious irony
that Lily, who once embodied the club's
motto: "We network hard, we play hard,"
was going to get Sidewaysed for doing
both. —Sure enough, a snafu was still taboo.
At exactly 12:30 p.m. on the second subsequent
Thursday, the verdict was sent—a Burgundy Fez
with a severed tassel. Everyone knew what that meant.

Warm Regards this Christmas

Della's gift of a vintage-car tree ornament
to each member of the department, while
a faux pas (we'd put a stop to secret Santas
years ago), seemed harmless. I put my gold
Model T in a drawer along with a mild pang
of guilt, and I would have forgotten about it,
if Seifert hadn't made Della's gift a moral
litmus test. "You'd think," he said,
"that a forty-five-year-old diabetic divorcee,
dependent on the health plan, pay cut and demoted,
just a hair's breadth from getting the chop
during lean times, might at least *pretend*
to acquire a work ethic. Instead she wastes
an entire day handing out ornaments."
Seifert smirked—"I get the Mercedes," he said,
raising his fingers for quote marks, "Because
I'm 'powerful yet whimsical.' She not
only lacks the discipline to save her money,
she lacks the guts to face responsibilities."

If you admitted the justice of his view,
Seifert went on, you believed that our lives
were not dictated by fate—that people had
free will and a responsibility to help
themselves. And he wasn't just talking;
he was willing to act. He would collect
the price of our ornaments from us and write
a check on Della's behalf to the gas company.
Marcie said that was rubbing Della's face in it
—that this was vintage victimization by modern
society. Jones said Marcie was just proud
of her Corvette because she was supposedly *sleek*
to the point of sinful, but classy in a rounded way.
(Jones himself got a Bug.) Leilany (a Jaguar)
said Della lacked the advantages we had,

including good taste. Seifert said that kind
of high-minded talk never got down far enough
to lace up boot-straps. —"What about you?"
he asked me. I wasn't an Edsel. I believed
in boot-straps and Ben Franklin. I chipped in
a couple of bucks. But I refused to sign his card
that read: "Warm Regards this Christmas."

Recipe for Disaster
as compiled by Lily Carmichael

Begin with the perfect job in an ideal office.

Add a heavy dose of ambition,
a half-ounce of prevention,
one basket of all the eggs
you count on hatching.
Breathe the heady smell of success.

This is called flirting.

Stir with the short end of the stick
until trouble brews.

Next comes one rock,
one hard place,
a little diced root of all evil,
a gallon of midnight oil.

By now, something should smell fishy.

Throw in a bone of contention
and a bunch of sour grapes,
but not yet the towel.

Wait for a second wind to fan the fire
until you smell desire burning its bridges.

Set your timetable to the point of no return,
expecting too much too soon.

Lastly, a straw.

Hooper on the Inside

After two months of high stakes and his
own slow reaction to them, Hooper got it.
The Enterprise audit wasn't a soap opera
after all. It was a sit-com, *starring Rich Kotch
as the punctilious Senior with a penchant
for pressure and a passion for acronyms.*
Seated at the MSS (Monday Strategy Session),
Hooper watched anew as Kotch turned
a plain, white flip-chart into a launching pad
for one-liners: URGNT ASSIGNS THS WK:
—Kraus: inventory from LIFO to FIF0
—Hooper: test the AP-SL EDP
—Taft: SOP for COD

Hooper couldn't resist elbowing Taft
in the ribs— "FYI he forgot ASAP."
Taft (to his credit) gave Hooper a puzzled
frown and stayed in character as *the crew's
straight-man with a flair for the deadpan.*
Taft was also a master of physical comedy:
storming loud-heeled across the carpet,
slamming down phones, jab-jab-jabbing
elevator buttons. And he was no slouch
with the sight gag: cylindrically starched
cuffs, braided leather suspenders, dimpled tie.
You could learn a lot from a pro like that.

But Hooper figured he'd get his laughs
as a writer. At his desk, he began a script
called *Departmental Travel Procedures*:
"~~According to~~ In accordance with
the new DTP rules, travel expenses
~~should meet~~ shall be recorded in a manner
consistent with the DT Finance Guide, and
Appendix O of the Joint Corporate / Subsidiary

Travel Regulations (JCTR/ JSTR). And
~~that's just for starters~~, prior to departure,
the traveler shall supply cost estimates
in compliance with Component Travel Regulation 35,
unless ~~get this~~ traveling internationally.
International travel requires that one submit
the following ~~mind-boggling~~ additional
items, including but not limited to . . ."
If he could just keep himself from cracking up,
Hooper was going to bring down the house.

Culture

While Gracie was in London, she sent
the department a post card every day:
Houses of Parliament, The Tower of London,
Buckingham Palace and the Changing
of the Guard. Dorma tacked them up
in the coffee room, and you could just imagine
Gracie strolling barefoot across Abbey Road,
eating fish and chips at a pub. Soaking up
all that culture. On the card with the word 𝕰𝖓𝖌𝖑𝖆𝖓𝖉
superimposed over the Union Jack, she wrote,
"To tell you the truth, chaps, I'm a little
overwhelmed. Say the word 'London'
and I picture a red double-decker bus
with oil paintings and horse statues sticking out
the windows. Cardboard beefeaters, the clock
arms of Big Ben, bobbies' helmets, rusty cannons,
and hundreds of swords all pouring out the doors.
Crown Jewels trickling down the street."
Leilany said, wasn't it just like Gracie
to make light of her amazing experience?
"It's true," I said, "there was always something
worldly about her." Leilany grew reflective.
"Was a time, before you got here, they allowed
us to hang posters on the cube walls. . . . I used to
have one of *Casablanca*, the movie. Big cabaret
with ceiling fans, Bogey in a trench coat
and fedora.   Tiny airplane lifting off in the fog."

Club Edge

Renee was always urging us bean-counters
to go clubbing instead of drinking at Crumley's
or The Ale House. So we finally met her at The Edge.
She wore torn leggings and thick eye-liner.
"Who're you supposed to be," said Duke—"a raccoon?"
"You all look like you came from work," she said,
frowning heaviest at Marcie's tan slacks
and penny loafers. The club was dark and strobing.
Frenetic synthesizers ricocheted off the walls.
We took our drinks to a landing overlooking the dance
floor. Suspended over the platform was a huge
birdcage with a skeleton gyrating inside it. Closer up,
you could see it was a woman wearing black leotards
with glow-paint flashing white-hot in the black light.
Duke said he'd like to jump her bones. We were excited.
We kept pointing out vampires and pale, dark-haired
sirens. But then, between songs, the skeleton
suddenly turned and banged the bars of her cage.
"If you're just going to stare," she shouted—"leave!"
Before I could think, Duke shot back, "Conformist!"
Just the kind of wit that normally occurs to you hours later,
driving-thru Two Pesos. What could she do but shoot
a boney finger and snarl her haughty black lips.
The music resumed, and Renee shouted something
at Duke and walked downstairs. We lost her
for the night, though we stayed a good hour and a half.

Later, after shots at Waves, driving-thru Two Pesos,
Duke said for the hundredth time that night:
"You see the look on Skeleton-Chick's face?—*Conformist!*
 Talk about lockjaw!" "Yeah," I mustered a chuckle—
"talk about rattling her cage." But it was late, and I had
that feeling of standing outside my life again. Duke snapped
off the radio. "What's Renee's problem, anyway?"
he said—"And what does she mean, *pyrrhic victory?*"
"It's late," I said—"Let's call it a night."

How Albert Wound Up at Enterprise, not Rice & Feller

Albert knew what Kent—the head-phone-
wearing, *Rolling Stone*-reading treasurer
of their honorary accounting fraternity,
Beta Alpha Psi—did not, that sitting in the back
of the Rice & Feller luxury charter bus,
they were pitching their job prospects
out the window like greasy cheeseburger
wrappers, leaving them to tumble behind
in Columbus where their grades had earned
them, like the others on this bus, early
consideration from one of the nation's best firms.

No mistake, this charter to Chicago was a rolling
stage, the first act of a weekend-long audition
for the part of the smart, motivated, people person,
and consequently also the well-paid college graduate.

So why wasn't he yucking it up like Tammy,
Carol, and Sam at the front of the bus
with the group from Cleveland, playing poker
with partner Jerry Clayborn, betting swizzle sticks,
drinking Bud Light? Why not give a hearty laugh
when Tammy's jokers-wild straight trumped
his pair of Jacks? "Read 'em and weep, guys!"
she'd just called out, swizzle stick in her teeth.

Yes, read 'em and weep, Albert thought.
Because it didn't matter if Tammy was bluffing
or not, so long as she kept up her enthusiasm.
He could read that much already. And for all
anyone knew, she might keep it up forever.

Those sudden moments of doubt that Albert
had begun calling his inner auditor had picked a fine
time to call his own bluff. What he would later dub
his piss-poor poker face was giving it all away.

Life After College

Carson asked me where a good hang out
place was in this town—not a dance club.
Somewhere casual but cool if I knew what he meant.
I felt honored. Renee was already calling
him the most eligible bachelor in the company.
Working on the flow chart project at HQ,
I found out this much: he graduated Tech,
full-ride on a rodeo scholarship. Ruptured
three disks just before turning pro. Studied
in his hospital bed, passed the CPA Exam first crack,
and signed with RKW. Made early senior
while plunged into a romantic intrigue
that involved a partner in Dallas before
ending up here. He carried only a thin briefcase
and he refused to have a ten key on his desk,
using an old Texas Instruments for the occasional
reasonableness test, leaving his staff
to crunch numbers and foot schedules.

Despite knowing this, I told him that Waves
on Westheimer was hot. Righteous,
if he knew what I meant. Later, I realized
how stupid that sounded. Waves, for godsakes!
Home of the fake palm tree and trucked-in
beach. Deck Parties packed with the young,
hard-rocking, hard-drinking professional set.
Here was a guy who wore cowboy boots
to the office, played guitar, chased models—a guy
who proved there was life after college. And
what do I suggest?—A damn time capsule.

To Staff

From Rich Kotch, Senior
Re: Raymond Hooper's Resignation

Yesterday, Ray Hooper informed me
that he has accepted a job at one of our
clients. He assured me his decision
to leave Dressel & Fitzweiller wasn't
personal but based on a need for flexible
hours, and he hoped his departure hasn't
left us in a bind. He agonized over
the pay cut and the great opportunities
he'll be throwing away, but the illusion
of control was too strong to pass up.
Those of us who've imagined the frightening
specter of mediocrity will, I am sure,
wish him the best in his struggle against it.
At exactly two o'clock, there will be a short
gossip period, after which the subject is off limits.

Tad Aldridge and the MS Walk-A-Thon

Sure he'd take part in the Walk-A-Thon
but he didn't like to sweat so he wasn't walking
or collecting pledges but he wanted the t-shirt
all the same—he just did—fifty bucks was fifty
bucks and if he wanted a commemorative t-shirt
(XL) that was his business take it or leave it
in fact leave it—forget you and your phony
do-good-a-thon but remember without him
you could kiss hundred percent participation
goodbye along with the plaque (signed by
the regional manager himself) awarded
to "team leaders" charismatic enough to rally
the whole department in a community-building
charity event—a feather—maybe *the* feather
in the cap of those on the march to early promotion.
Who should he make out the check to?

Chief Counsel, Bart Coughlin, Vs. The Aphids
as performed by Renee Turner

"You need a thick skin down here in legal
I can tell you. A goddamn exoskeleton,
you understand? A-hem. Two hundred
eco-protesters sue us each year. Only
two make it to litigation. Nyang, a-hem.
Pardon me. For thirteen years—thirteen
years my desk has been the leaf where
environmentalists have come to feed nyang
on the company's retained earnings.
I've had to be as ravenous as a lady bug,
nyang, deposing and debunking every
preposterous entomologist with nyang
a clipboard, every camera-carrying college
professor who thinks she can parade nyang
around the property in the name of bug welfare.
*Lights, Camera, Aphids! It's always Lights,
Camera Aphids!* Ahem. I don't care,
nyang, how small the bite into our profits.
I don't care how beautiful, nyang,
and sensible the Joyce Cabbot nyang Ph.D.s.
A-hem. Show any weakness, nyang,
and they'll eat you nyang alive nyang.

Invasion of the Topless Dancers

Albert began dating a stripper named Shalimar
and running around with Arun and his BMW-driving
buddies from Dubai. After he'd phoned in sick
two Mondays in a row—still drunk—I said
his so-called *Arabian Nights* were fast becoming
a cautionary tale: *How I Wrecked My Career
and Why*. So I felt strangely relieved when
he said he needed just one more week to straighten
himself out. But that was the week he interviewed
at *Caligula's Cabaret* for the job of emcee.
Caligula's!—home of the two-song table dance.
As Albert told it later, it took the manager, Danny-O,
all of thirty seconds to see he was clueless
at the light board. But apparently Danny-O said
he did have a flair for punching phrases. He gave
Albert his card and told him to come back after some
soul-searching and, more importantly, practice.
After that, Albert settled down. It seemed enough,
somehow, to have Danny-O's card, which he laminated
and carried like a magic password, proof, he said,
that he was a CPA with some uncertainty left
in his future. We all said he was crazy. Then,
for weeks, in rush hour traffic, I found myself
reading billboards for places like Rick's: The Finest
Gentlemen's Club in Texas. I'd slip in an old Heart
CD and work the volume at the introduction, saying
in this new, deep, voice, "All Riiiight, Gentlemen!
MmmmmAKE some NOISE! Coming straight onto you
—the GORgeous, SEXy Sah-LEE-NAAAA!"

The UnAmerican Dream of Paul Martinez

He is falling from grace—behind friends
and enemies. Worse off than his parents
ever were. At rock bottom—a marble
committee room. Tall leather seats,
microphones, suspicious Senators. "Rise,"
says one. "Close your eyes. Touch a finger
to your nose and count your first million
backwards." He remains silent. Last act
as his own boss; first as agent of the state
of mind where nothing is possible.

Confidence Man

"Confidence!" said Brewer, my performance
consultant—"Let me hear a big hay-ell yeahhhhh!"

"I'm sorry," I said—"but the S-H-O-U-T method
just isn't me. *Shake it, Hustle, Overachieve*, all that."

"Insist on *can't* with a capital C, and you'll birth your limitations.
Believe in *Dreams* with a capital D, and live your *expectations*."

"I'm sorry," I said—"but remember when I broke
my leg trying a 360 in your *No Boundaries* ski-camp?"

"Man, you were *this* close to pulling it off.
You must have stopped believing, last second."

Razzmatazz

"I sell sales to salesmen, to salesmen I sell sales.
I sell sales to salesmen, to salesmen I sell sales,"
mumbled the man across the aisle from Rhonda Chung
on flight 584. "I sell sales to salesmen, to salesmen—"
He caught sight of Rhonda, cleared his throat,
and said, by way of apology, "It's a tongue
twister." Now she recognized him as
Melvin Brookline, author of the international
bestseller *The Six Factors of Success*.
"You're the greatest motivational speaker
of our generation," she said. "Razzmatazz,"
he huffed. "But I've read your book. It's brilliant!"
"Razzmatazz. What's *The Six Factors*, jacket blurbs
aside, but the message *you're okay*, dressed up
in the pinstripe suit of my Metro-Corp days
and repeated with inane clichés? 1. you're 100% fine;
2. thumbs up; 3. green light; 4. endorsed; 5. cleared
for take off; 6. go ahead, make your month."
He opened one of three remaining bottles of gin—
"Like I said, Razzmatazz." "Good enough for me
to become the top producer in my office,"
Rhonda said—"Mr. Brookline, you're the man
who proved that the self-disgusted cold-caller
in the boiler room doesn't need *strategy*.
She needs the same thing as the antacid-chewing
top-performer on vacation in the Bahamas
—to know that selling is okay. . . . And you
said it as eloquently as it's ever been said.
So I tip my cap to you, Mr. Brookline, and say,
You're okay. You're a 100% fine."

Down to Earth, Albert Reports on the Effects of Weightlessness

Without a center
         of gravity

      once weighty
ambitions   hang

     suspended
in airy encapsulation

         drifting over
experiment logs

bumping
porthole-magnificent

against a glittery world
     of might-have-beens

through which you streak
    open-mouthed

    curious
more than shocked

    light
       as a failure.

Bill-Paying Zombie

Seifert started paying his bills during lunch.
He sat in his usual place at the head of Lonny's
conference table, with his usual turkey on rye
and coffee, but now his checkbook. Mortgage,
electric, insurance, *National Geographic*.
It was a little rude. "You see McGee's catch
in the ninth last night?" I'd ask. —"Me? Nope."
"Going fishing this weekend?" —"Maybe."
Not that he was a great conversationalist, but he
could be counted on for the well-timed wise crack.
The humorous absurdity from the neighborhood.
Now, he was a bill-paying zombie. "Wish you were
that focused on your accounts," Lonny said
and cleared his throat.

From bills, Seifert moved to owner's manuals:
lawn-mower, attic fan, the car. "Did you know,"
he said, in a rare gregarious moment, "that modifying
your car with, say, a tachometer, voids the warranty?"
"Fascinating," Dorma said, her hands to her cheeks.
"You'll appreciate this, Dorma," Seifert went on, "You
can double the life of your tires if you maintain proper
air pressure and a strict rotating schedule. Double."
That was too much for Karmody. He pushed away
from the table and left muttering. But the next day,
Karmody was back—with a thick mutual fund prospectus.
"I never read these damn things," was all he said.

That left Lonny, Dorma and me on the other side
of the table with our sandwiches and our pride,
sweating under the pressure of coupons that could
be clipped, vehicles that could be balanced, bodies
that could be toned. "The French work only
thirty-five hours a week," Dorma bravely asserted—
"and take an entire month for holiday. In Paris

last summer all Gracie saw were tourists."
"We can all find great consolation in the French,"
said Seifert. Karmody chuckled behind his brochure
for steel gutters: "What's for lunch, Foie gras? Escargot?"

To lighten things up, Dorma made a soufflé for just
Lonny and me. It was delicious, but she ruined it
by saying, nonchalantly, as if just off the top
of her head while looking at her silver forks,
"Might have to bring my polish tomorrow."
Which she did. And between her polish
and the gasoline from the chainsaw carburetor
Lonny unfolded from a wad of newspaper,
my sandwich tasted like turpentine. I stood
and no one so much as glanced when I said
I was going for a walk. There they all were,
shoulder to shoulder, like some assembly-line
gone wrong, each tooling part of a contraption
that would never fit properly together.

The Life and Times of Jay Brewer, Performance Consultant

Based on the true story of a man
who based his life on the illusion
that dreams were an anvil, willpower
a hammer, and reality the stuff
in between. A man who re-forged
all evidence to the contrary in the dazzling
manner by which he would achieve
his dream of wealth and fame
telling others how it was done.

Another Work Dinner, Lonny Reflects

There he was in his good-sport coat,
raising a glass to Tilton's latest promotion,
surprising easily ("No. Really?") when it turned
out Gloria was right about third-quarter gains
all along. Eyes up, fork down, asking Harry
to tell the one about Harold the Great, returned
from his conquest of China and Hong Kong.

Here he was now, collar undone, coat hung
up, reflecting on the picture of sincerity
in the full-length mirror. Ambitious heart
pinned to his sleeve like a cuff-link.

The Loop

When it got bad, Albert told me,
he would buy a six of beer, crank up
Hank Williams, and drive the great 610
Loop around the city. Not so much
to outrun his demons as to corral them
for breaking later. Meanwhile, his father's
ghost would scale the Transco Tower
just west of The Loop and stagger on top
with a quart of whiskey, throwing tomatoes
at Albert. The same tomatoes that had rotted
when their vines weren't tied properly
that one of a dozen similar summers.

In The Era of Flex Time

Jones was the only one to choose a nine
to five-thirty shift. So when the office cleared
at 4:00 pm., an occasional manager would see
him at his desk or in the halls, smile, and say
to himself, *now there's someone who knows how
to grab a pie chart by the slice.* It went on
like this for two employee-of-the-month awards
before Dorma blew the whistle on a smoke break:
"I wouldn't exactly call it work," she told Lonny—
"And it's not exactly overtime." The next morning,
long before Jones got there, they rifled his cubicle
and found a stack of romance novels highlighted
in shipping-blue and invoice-green. That, more
than anything, ushered in the era of oversight
and production quotas. Naturally, the demise of flex
time. Oddly enough, the custom of casual dress
on Friday remained, and it was not uncommon
those days to see Jones wearing thin, loose-fitting,
pinstriped trousers with an elastic waistband. Along
with a matching v-neck sweater, the outfit could
have been construed as pajamas—or prison stripes,
depending on where you stood with management.

Sunday Afternoon

Dorma groaned when the doorbell buzzed
below. Her neighbor, come to recruit Dorma
for the block party. Now, the green cockatoo
of her latest greeting card would have to wait
for its tail feathers until the kids were in bed,
the income projections finished. Again the buzzer.
She struck her drafting table, then threw up
her hands. Just as quickly, she was struck
by the melodrama of her gesture.. Why were *these*
hours suddenly such costly casualties?

Hadn't she stood by calmly many times—
waving, even as in a parade—while regiments
of young hours marched to their certain end
in frivolous campaigns? This morning's coffee
and oranges on the sun porch, for instance.
Yet there were her aspirations crying *Liberté,*
égalité, fraternité, only to be blindfolded
—shoved into the courtyard as the blade rose
high in the smoke. She took a deep breath.
Would she go down with dignity?

Mayday

Looking back, you could read answers into
the question mark Renee made with silver
tacks stuck into her cubicle partition early
that May. And Aldy's mix of punk rock
classics, *Doc Marten Stomp*, copied and recopied,
will go down as the inflammatory soundtrack
of that weird summer when Jones was calling
us conformists and Albert was calling in sick.
Aldy, of course, was no punker and would
deny any part in Renee's *Theater of the Absurd*
(her impersonations of management and the spoofs
they inspired from a growing troupe of critics).
"She jaded us," Marcie would say, under pressure
in Lonny's office. And that was partly true.
Everything had become a joke to Renee, even
her own "ledgerized" life. She'd read memos
from the CEO as love letters to herself:
Dear Renee . . . Dearest Renee . . . Renee, my Love,
Third quarter results, though poorer than expected,
include several hopeful signs of robust recovery.
It made you feel something was wrong
with you too. The more earnest, the more lost.

For manager Lonny Harper it was simple:
Renee was poisoning the department.
Why start lunching in the park, for example,
except to say things unfit for the ears of the cafeteria?
(He seems not to have questioned cafeteria culture,
such as it was in those days.) In retrospect,
Lonny's demotion of his only brilliant auditor
topped off a season of deepening mistrust
and shifting loyalties. Didn't it confirm something?
Something now that could never be undone?
Oh, Renee. Oh, to be back then, early May—
before Marcie would report unrest

in the park—wasn't it possible, then, to read
Renee's question mark as a salute to youth
and idealism by a woman in her mid-twenties
with (even as she, herself, must have understood it)
a promising career with us at Enterprise?

Departmental

Sure enough, on November fifth a bouquet
of gardenias and snap dragons with baby's
breath appeared on Seifert's credenza.
We razzed him about his secret admirer.
But of course the flowers were for Jerry.
They'd shown up at his former cube five years
now on the anniversary of his heart attack
when, purple faced and wild-eyed, he lurched
up from his chair, "clutching a fountain pen,"
as the story had it, before collapsing
stone dead. No one knew who she was,
this mysterious lady, who had once again
drawn a lipstick heart on the beige felt
of Jerry's old cube—in protest, no doubt,
of the departmental policy against dating
co-workers that had forced their affections
underground. We liked thinking of Jerry
(who'd never married or taken good care
of himself and seemed quietly resigned to fate)
as a writer of love notes and planner of illicit
rendezvous. "Here's to old Casanova,"
Seifert said, lifting his coffee cup.
Gracie raised her Diet Coke with a fierce,
distant smile—"Dirty old men need love, too."

Renee Departs

After her farewell luncheon, Renee
got up and thanked us for a memorable
five years. She'd miss us, but she owed
it to herself to explore new possibilities.
"Like what?" asked Dorma, impressed
but suspicious. "Well, for starters, you
might say I'm getting off the success train
and going for a long walk in the woods."
"In your high heels?" someone kidded.
We were going to miss Renee. We all
said so. We followed her as far
as the foyer and watched her walk onto
the blacktop and out of our lives, possibly
forever, waving goodbye as she strode
down what we all worried was the fast-closing
path to our own true selves. Then, Lonny
called out: "All Aboard!" And we turned,
churning slowly, picking up speed.

Charles Sweetman teaches writing at Washington University in St. Louis. His chapbook manuscript *Incorporated* won the 2007 Dream Horse Press Chapbook Prize. He has published numerous essays, poems, and stories including the chapbook *Lake House and Other Stories*. His fiction and poetry have appeared in such places as *River Styx*, *GSU Review*, and *Poet Lore*.

www.ingramcontent.com/pod-product-compliance
Lightning Source LLC
Chambersburg PA
CBHW022030090426
42739CB00006BA/367